GUSTAVE CAILLEBOTTE COLORING BOOK

---

24 Masterpieces by Caillebotte

FREDERIC DURAND

"The world is but a canvas to our imagination."
—Henry David Thoreau

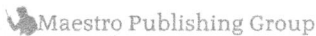Maestro Publishing Group

Pubished by Maestro Publishing Group

Commentary by Anna Krutiy.

Printed in the United States of America
ISBN: 978-1619494855

CONTENTS

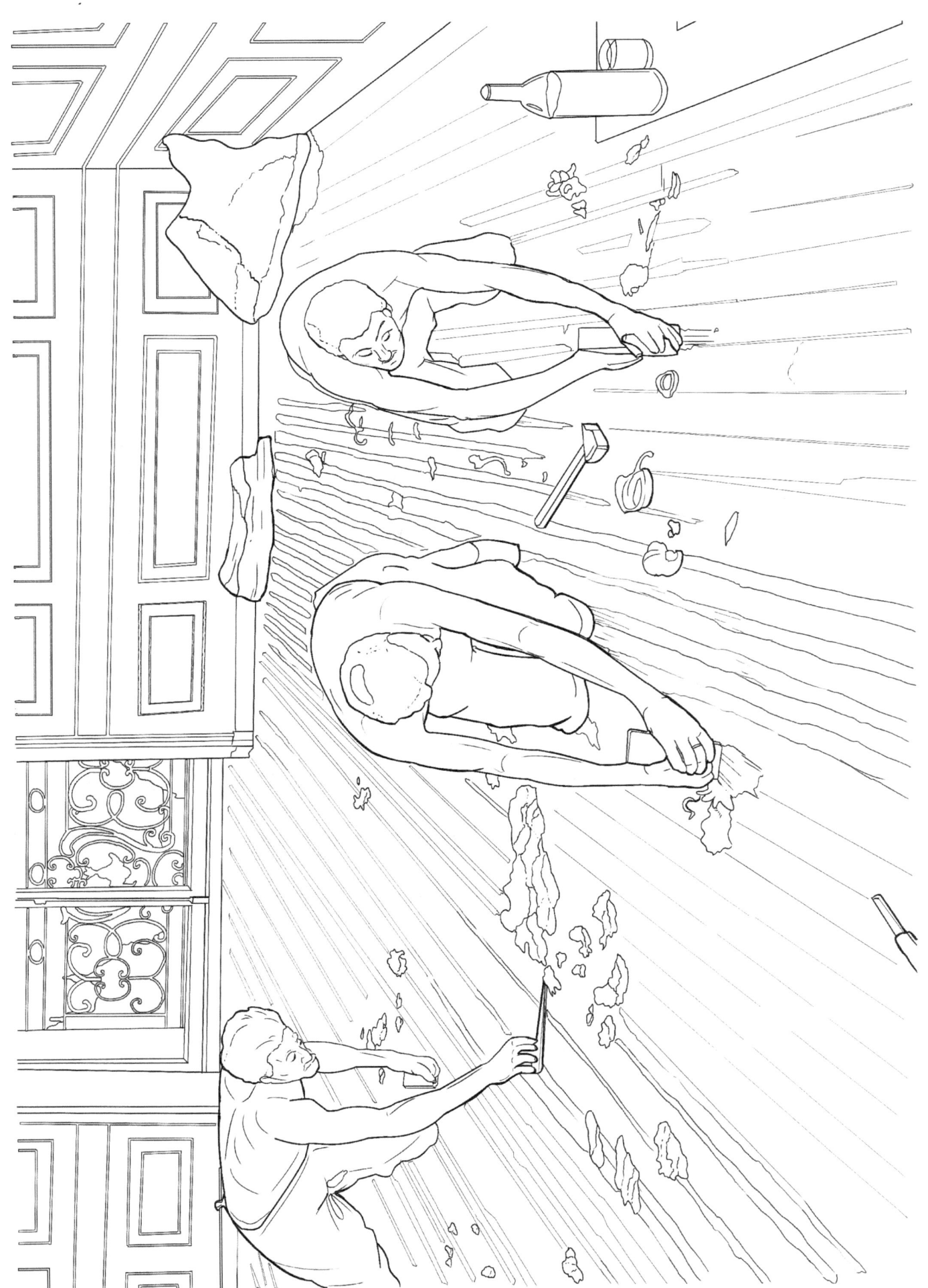

3

Plate 1.
The Floor Scrapers, 1875.

This painting, one of the most famous works of Caillebotte, portrays an image of the laborers' world during the 19th century modern Paris and the industrial revolution. The workers are scraping the floors in a Hotel Particulier in Paris on Rue de Miromesnil, owned by the artist's father. The realistic subject matter was at the time considered by many vulgar, in a parallel way as the literature of Zola, who described everyday life scenes of ordinary laborers working in factories, miners, railmen, plumbers or laundry workers.

The nude torsos showing prominent reliefs of the worker's vertebrae, muscular shoulders and slender arms, recall that the artist has studied classical anatomy at the atelier of Bonnat. The faces of the workers are hidden or are partially hidden, the viewer's attention is thus concentrated on the task of the workers and on their hard physical labor, which is the main subject of the painting. The only objects around also belong to the worker's trade : hammer, filing instruments, wood planes, a glass bottle. The absence of the ceiling focus the viewer's eyes on the floor, as if we are to feel the same view and atmosphere that the workers are immersed into. The linear perspective of the wooden planks and the bright light reflections direct our gaze directly to the worker's bodies.

Outside the window, we can notice some typical Parisian roofs, a theme that is later developed in the artist's works.

This painting was donated to the national museums by the artist's heirs in 1894 and can now be seen in Impressionism Museum Orsay.

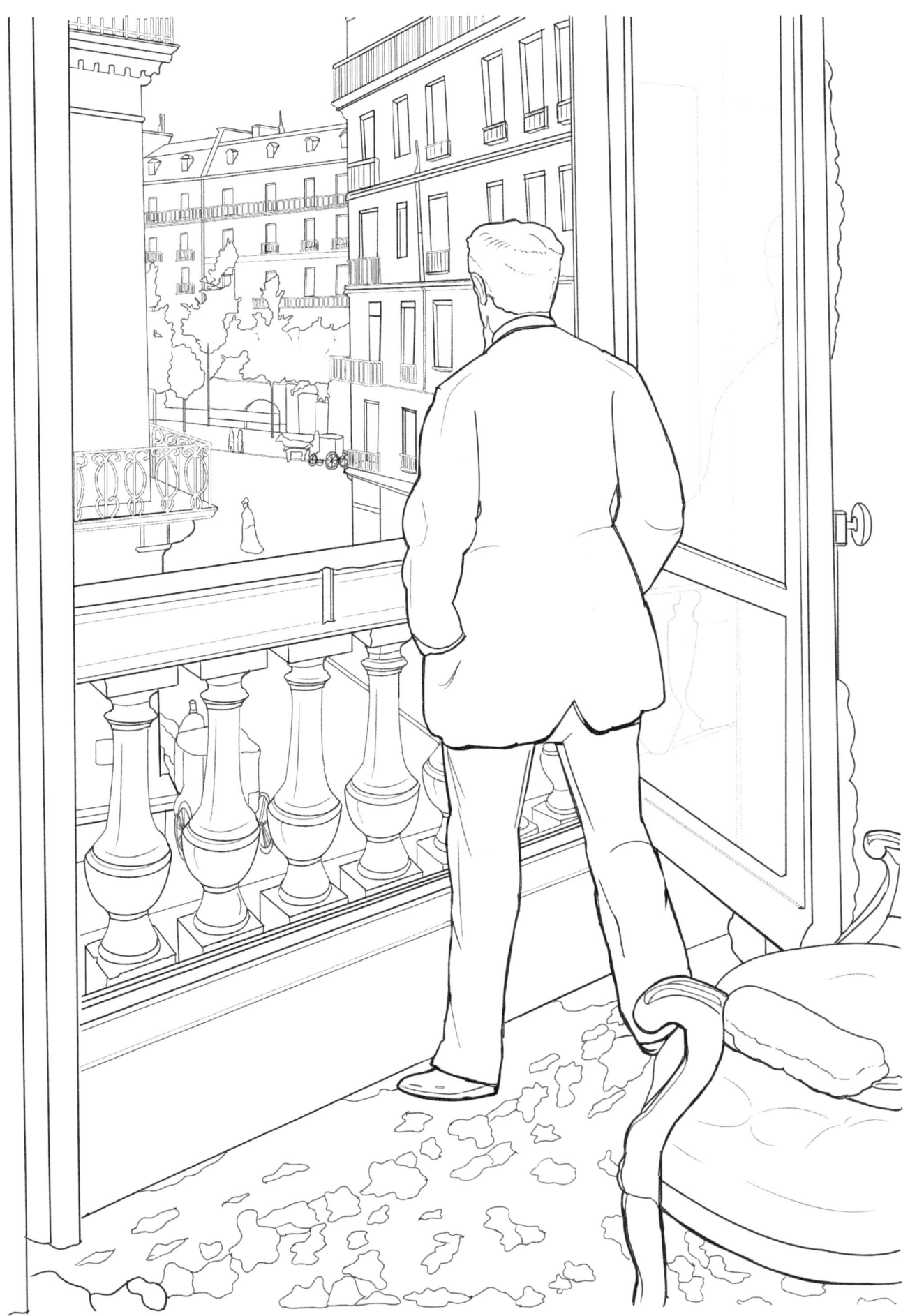

Plate 2.
Young Man At His Window, 1875.

"Looking from outside into an open window one never sees as much as when one looks through a closed window... What one can see out in the sunlight is always less interesting than what goes on behind a windowpane. In that black or luminous square life lives, life dreams, life suffers. " The windows, as in the poem of the same title by a French poet Baudelaire, along with balconies, were one of the recurrent and symbolic themes of Caillebotte's paintings. Baudelaire's poetry and prose, describing the ever changing nature of beauty and the modern experience of urban city life, has inspired and influenced many prominent writers and artists of the time, who felt responsible for capturing their fleeting moments in the modern metropolis. For Caillebotte, the windows were an expression of the world that could be shared equally with his wealthy family and with his less fortunate artist friends.

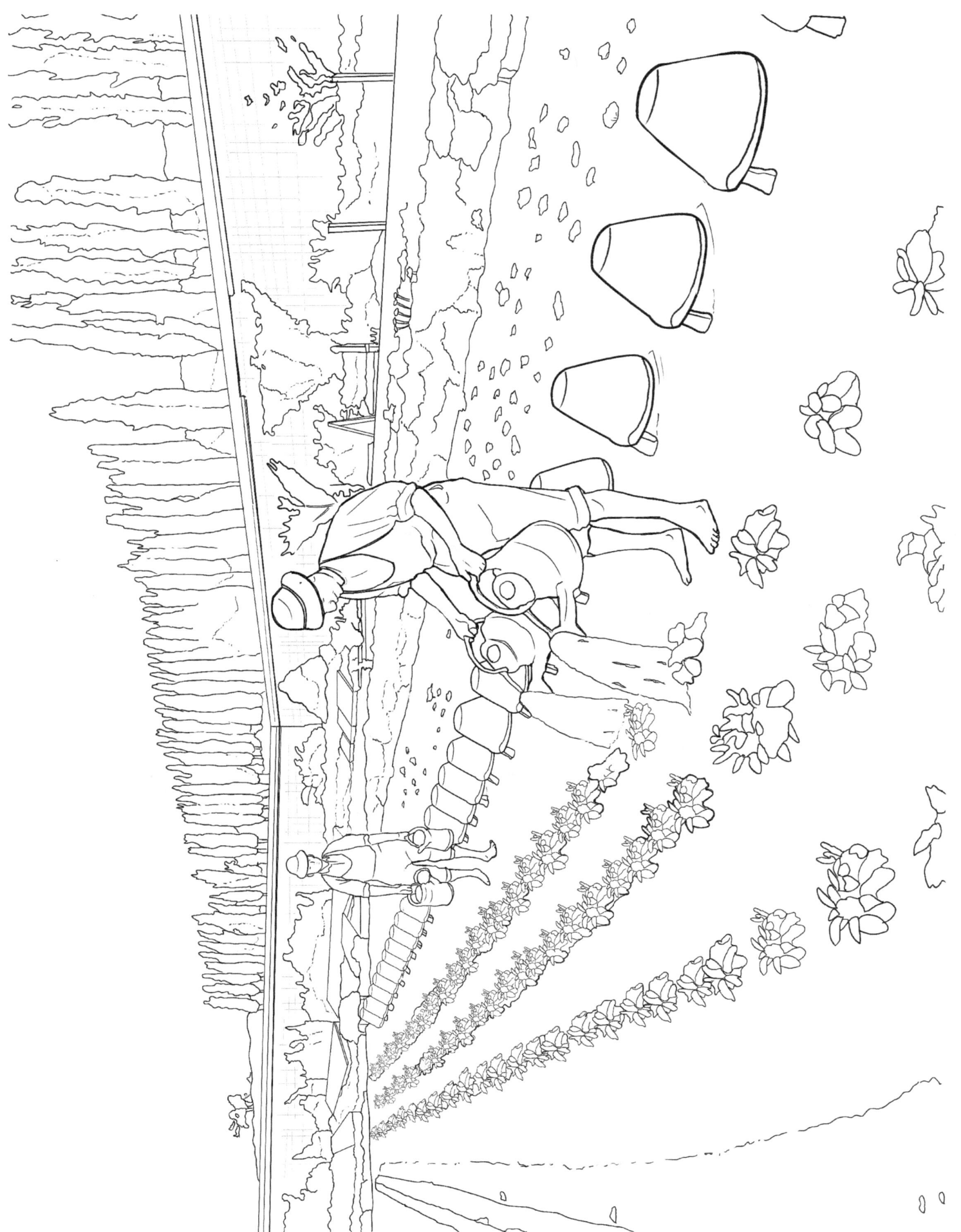

Plate 3.
The Gardeners, 1875-77.

When Caillebotte was 12 years old, his family moved to the large estate at Yerres, which was crucial for the artist's pictorial inspiration and evolved his passion for nature. The surface of the gardens was more than 5500 m2 and five gardeners were employed to take care of the vast territory. Caillebotte has painted several works that depicted the everyday life of workers in the gardens.

As his close friend Monet, who owned a large estate and a beautiful flower gardens with lily ponds at Giverny, Caillebotte was passionate about gardening and horticulture, the science and art of producing and improving flowers, fruits, vegetables and ornamental plants. The artist's vivid interest in gardening was later confirmed by the numerous letters he has shared with Monet on the subject of horticulture and rare plants such as orchids and poppies. Caillebotte often visited his friend's estate in Giverny and the artist's passion for gardening and flowers is further confirmed by numerous paintings with still life flowers and fruits.

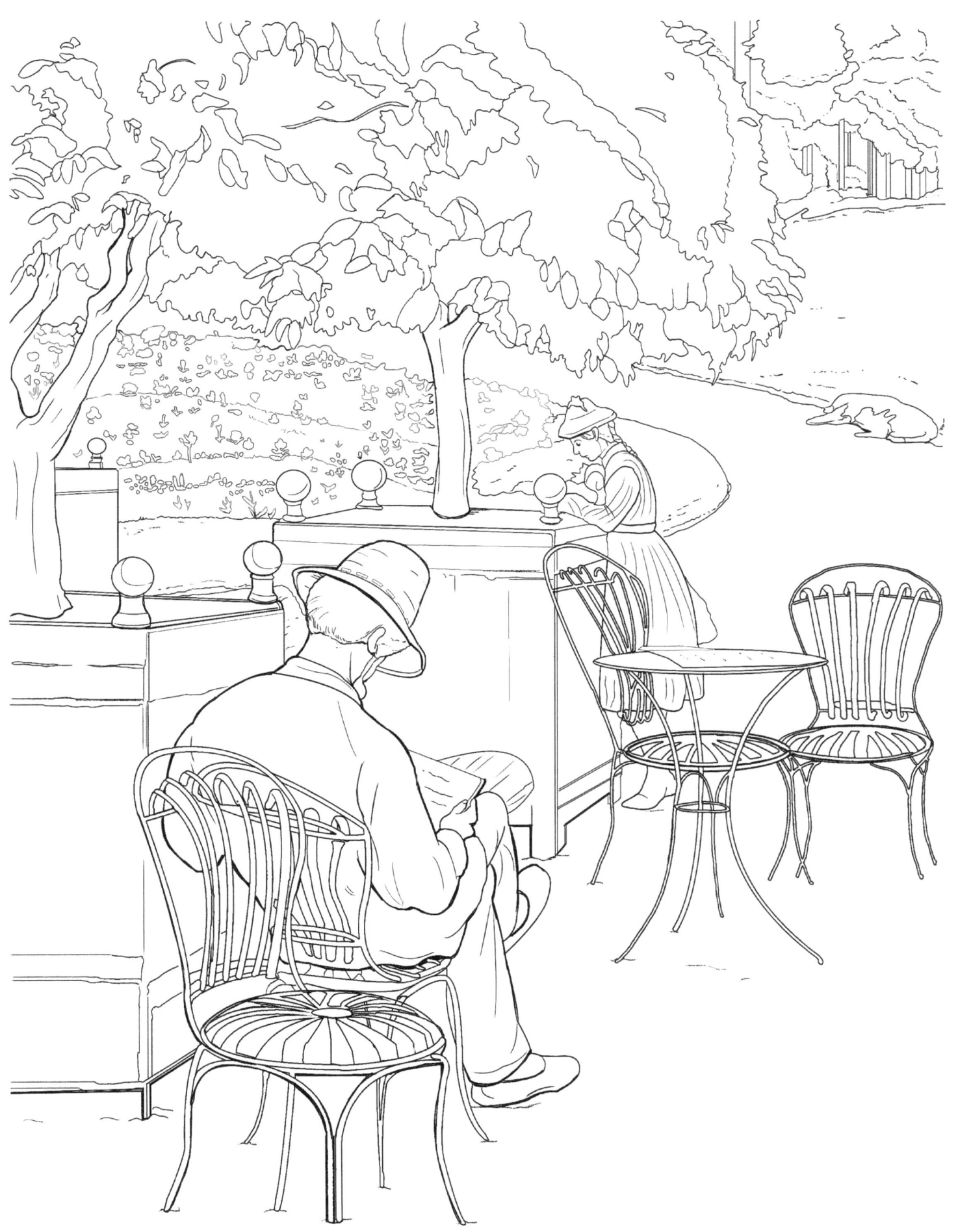

Plate 4.
The Orange Trees, **1878.**

The orange trees in this painting are situated in a park belonging to the Yerres domain. At the time when Caillebotte finished this painting, he already possessed Claude Monet's famous painting The Lunch (Le Dejeneur) in his collection. As in Monet's painting, Caillebotte shows the spontaneity of a moment, playing with the contrasting bright light and the effects of the shadows. The theme of the painting are simple and quiet moments of domestic and family life. A man is leisurely reading in the shade of the orange trees foliage, while a female figure in the background is attentively nursing a baby.

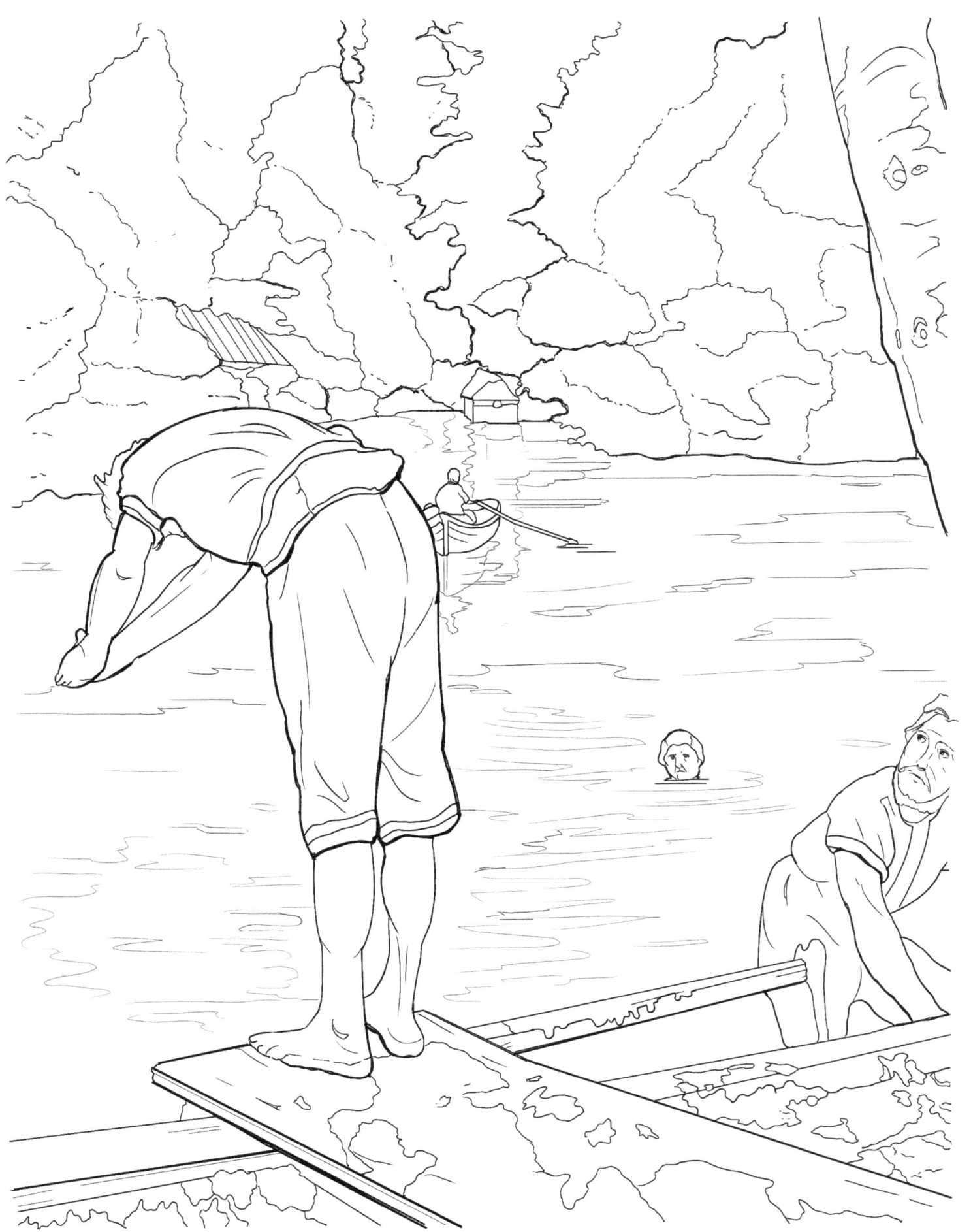

11

Plate 5.
Bather Preparing to Dive, **1877.**

This painting is one of the three in the series of a decorative cycle *Baigneurs* that Caillebotte depicted on the bank of the Yerres river. The scene is situated at Caillebotte's family summer residence in Yerres and shows a swimmer preparing to dive into the refreshing water. The artist depicts this charming scene in an almost anecdotal way in its naturalistic expression and bold simplicity. The moving figures are depicted in a fleeting moment, as if to immortalize a passing instant. This new technique was going against the academic tradition and used often by Caillebotte who immortalized his family and friends visiting the estate at Yerres.

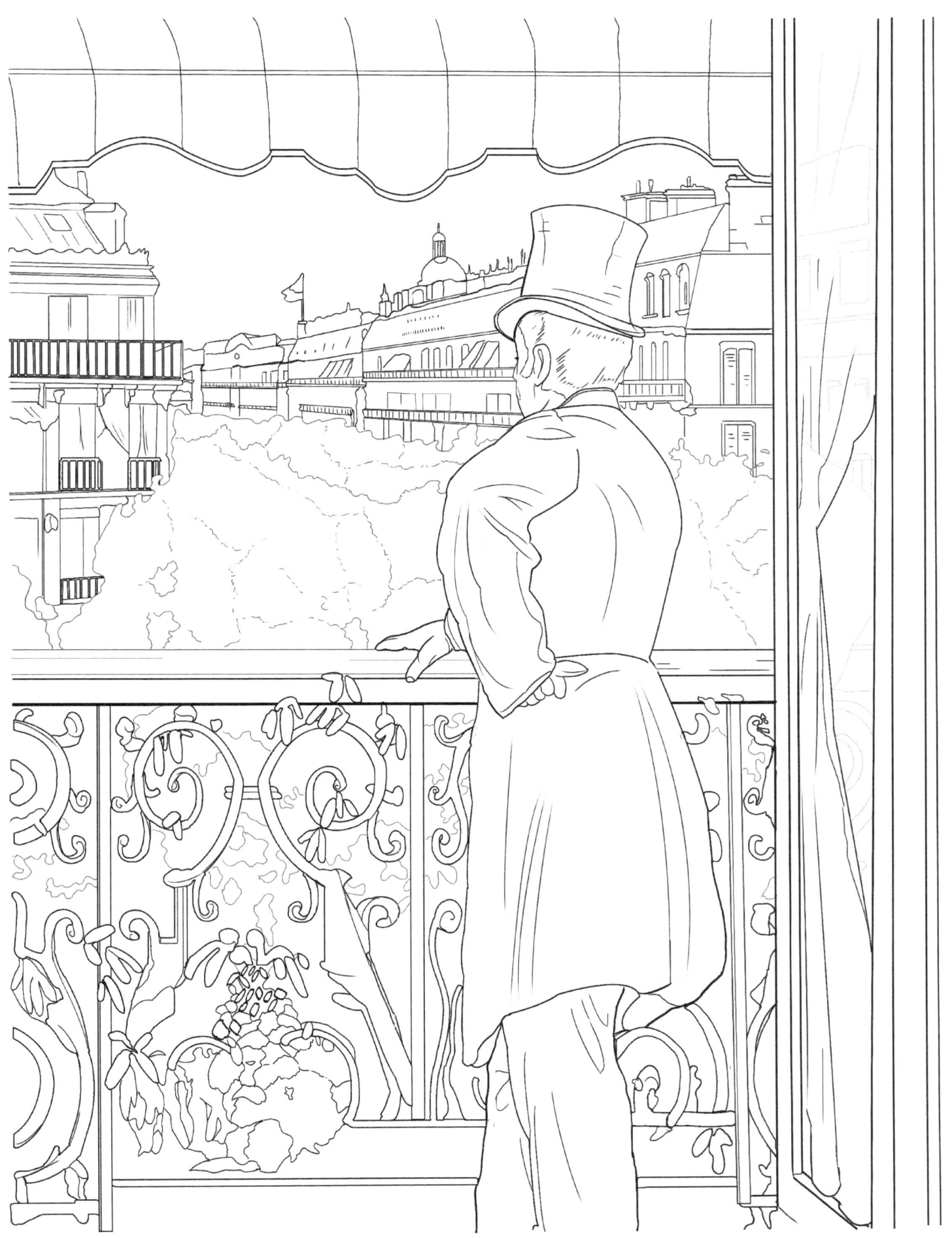

Plate 6.
A Man at the Balcony, Boulevard Haussmann, **1880.**

Caillebotte painted different versions of the *Homme au balcon*. The original perspective and the vanishing point catches the viewer's eye directing the gaze outside to the Haussmann Paris. Here we witness again the recurring theme of windows and balconies favored by the artist. The protagonist in a top hat and a fashionable upper-class suit is immersed in the grandiosity of the exterior space. Outside we can witness the tree lined Haussmann Boulevard and the modern vast space that has opened up after the reconstruction of Paris. Haussmann Paris, a modern city plan that is modeled on a symmetrical and geometrical grid, dividing the medieval scattered Paris into neatly planned arrondissements and districts, is also one of the favorite and recurring scenes in Caillebotte's paintings.

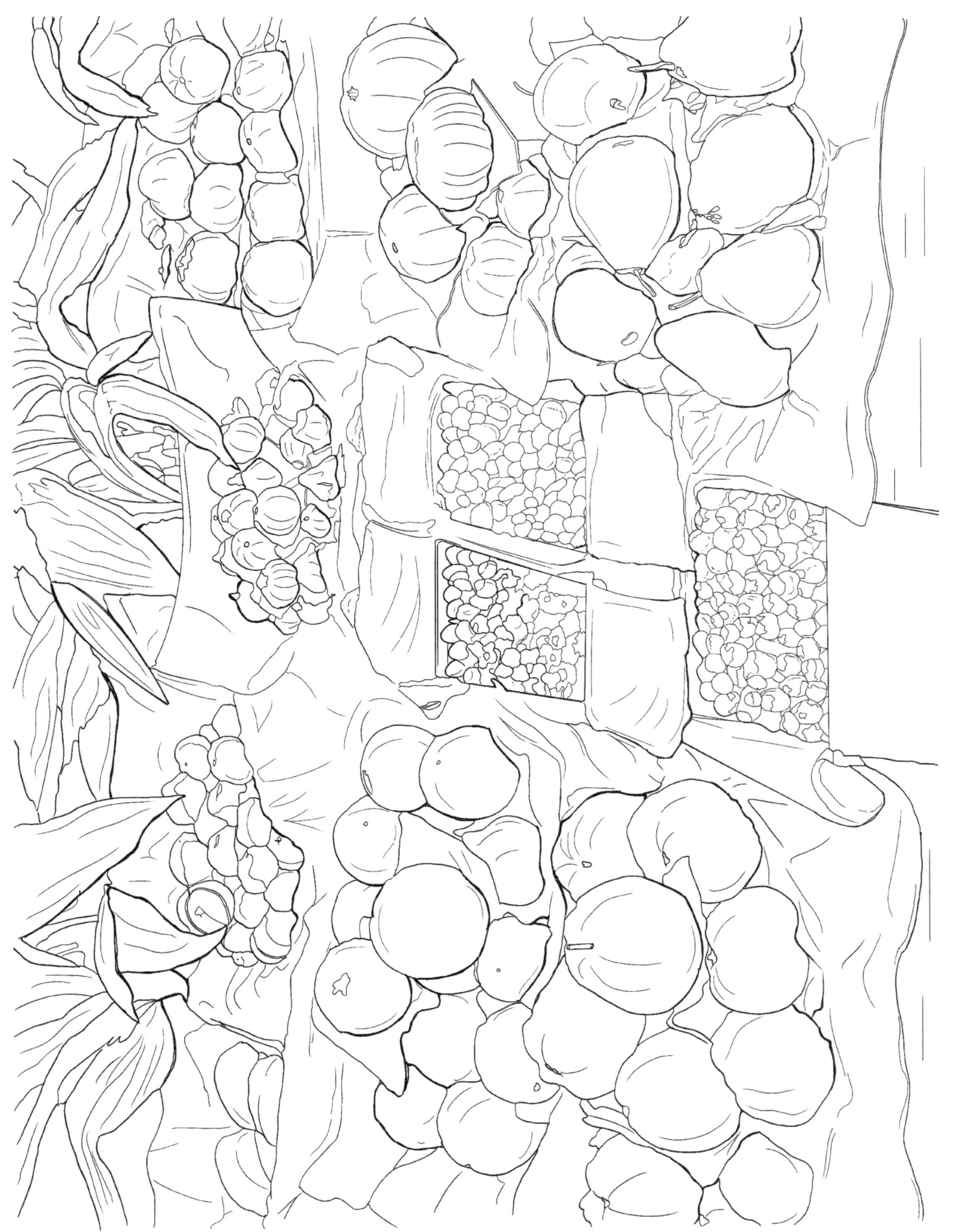

Plate 7.
Fruits displayed on a stand, **1881.**

This painting belongs to important still life compositions executed for the main part between 1881-1882. The close-up view of seasonal fruits stacked up on a market display are painted with great attention to detail and to the reflection of light, creating bold patterns of bright and vivid colors. The painter depicts the fruits as if they were cushioned sparkling colored gemstones on a vendor's stand. The sensual brushstrokes suggest the juiciness and ripeness of the fruits. This painting is reminiscent of the fruit and flower gardens of the painter as well as his passion for the horticulture. The work was destined to decorate a dining room of the artist's friend Monsieur Albert Courtier, a notary in Meaux.

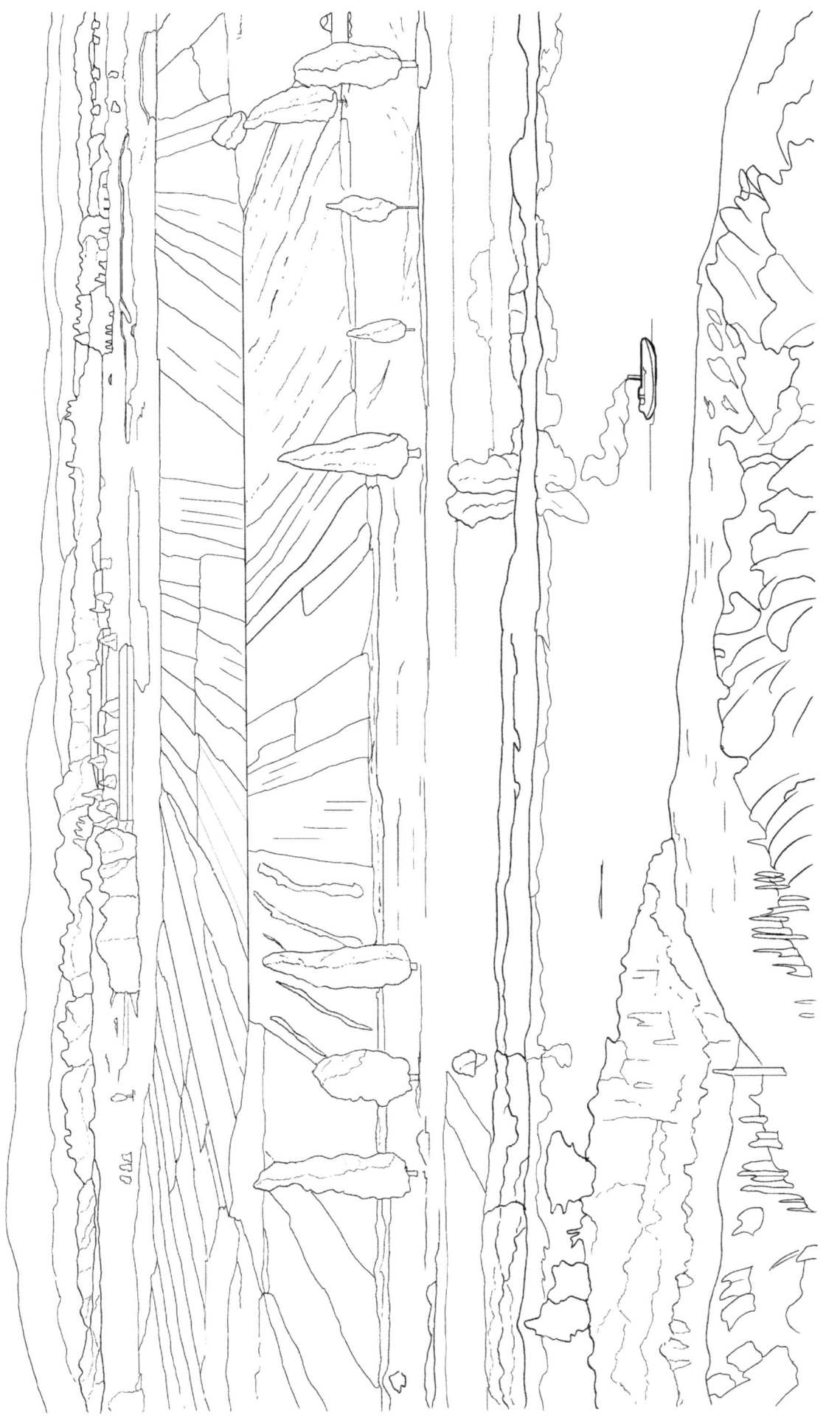

Plate 8.
The Plain of Gennevilliers, **1884-88.**

This work is a part of series of six paintings depicting Gennevilliers plains, planted with vegetables, which were adjacent to the artist's property at Petit Gennevilliers. The property was situated on the banks of the Seine River across from Argenteuil, half an hour's train ride away from Paris. The artist purchased a property and a country house there with his brother Martial in 1881. The view is close to a birds-eye-view and is executed from the Hills of Argenteuil.

In this painting we can witness Caillebotte's fascination with nature and beauty of the colorful harvests. The artist's passion for perspective, structure and organization of his canvases, is evident here by the sharp diagonal lines and simplified geometric patterns of the repeating rows with planted vegetables and flowers, dispersed in different directions. Caillebotte makes this painting full of life and dynamic movement, despite the lack of human moving figures, applying think layers of creamy yellow, pink, burnt sienna, blue and green dashes of brushstrokes.

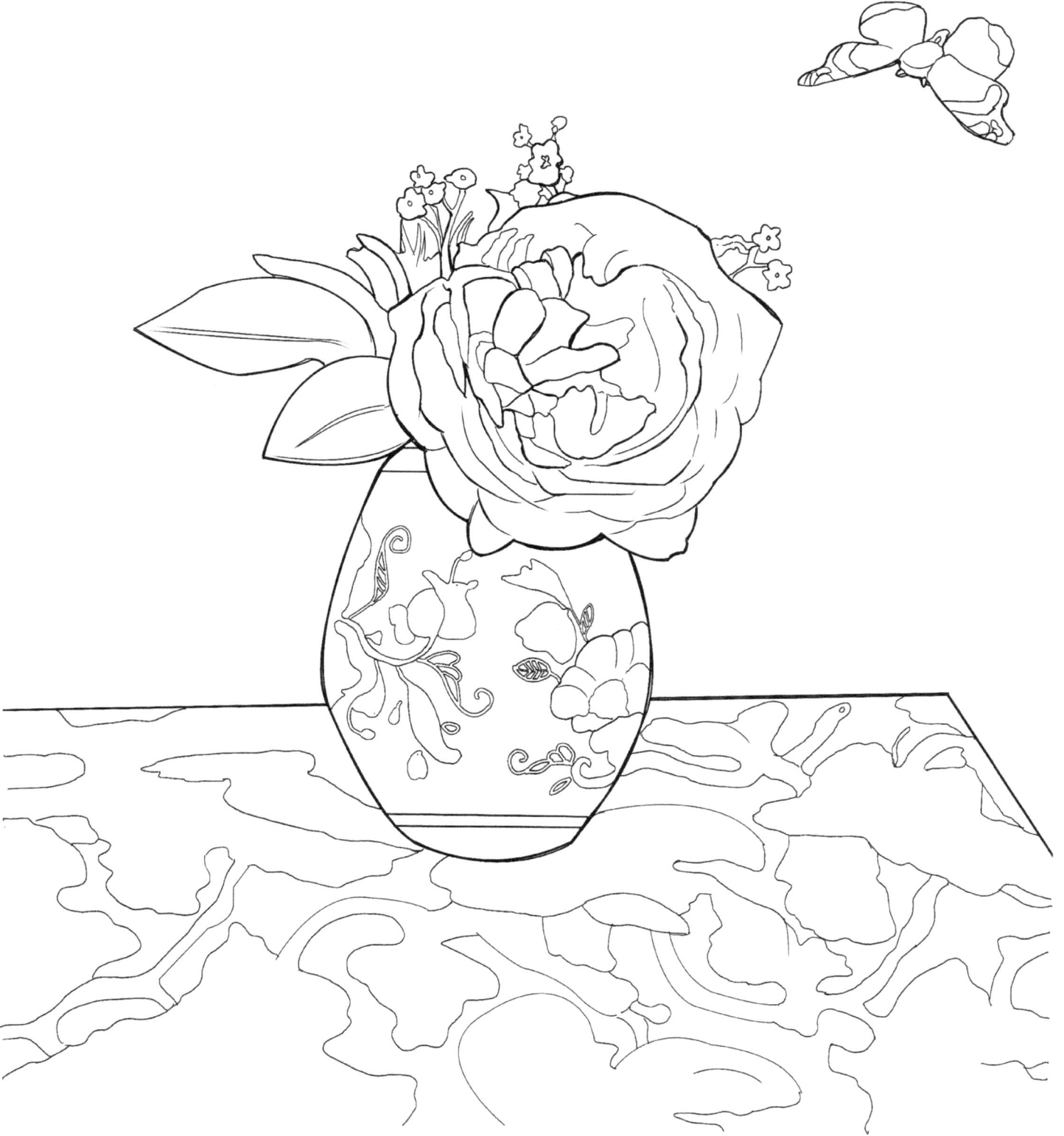

Plate 9.
Garden Rose and Blue Forget-me-nots in a vase, **1878.**

A small bouquet of delicate forget-me-nots and one fully bloomed creamy red rose is set on a red patterned drapery against a hazel green background. This simple but charming still life most likely depicts a flower composition from the artist's own garden. Caillebotte was greatly interested in the renewed genre of still life and has painted numerous paintings in this genre. As in several other still lives with flowers, Caillebotte masterfully plays with the contrast between the minimalistic composition and the highly detailed rose in the center. The red flower and the foliage pattern is repeated throughout the painting, as we can see it echoed on the vase design, and again on the flower patterned luxurious table cloth. Even the bright red stripes and tiny white dots on the butterfly's wings seem to mirror this wave-like floral pattern.

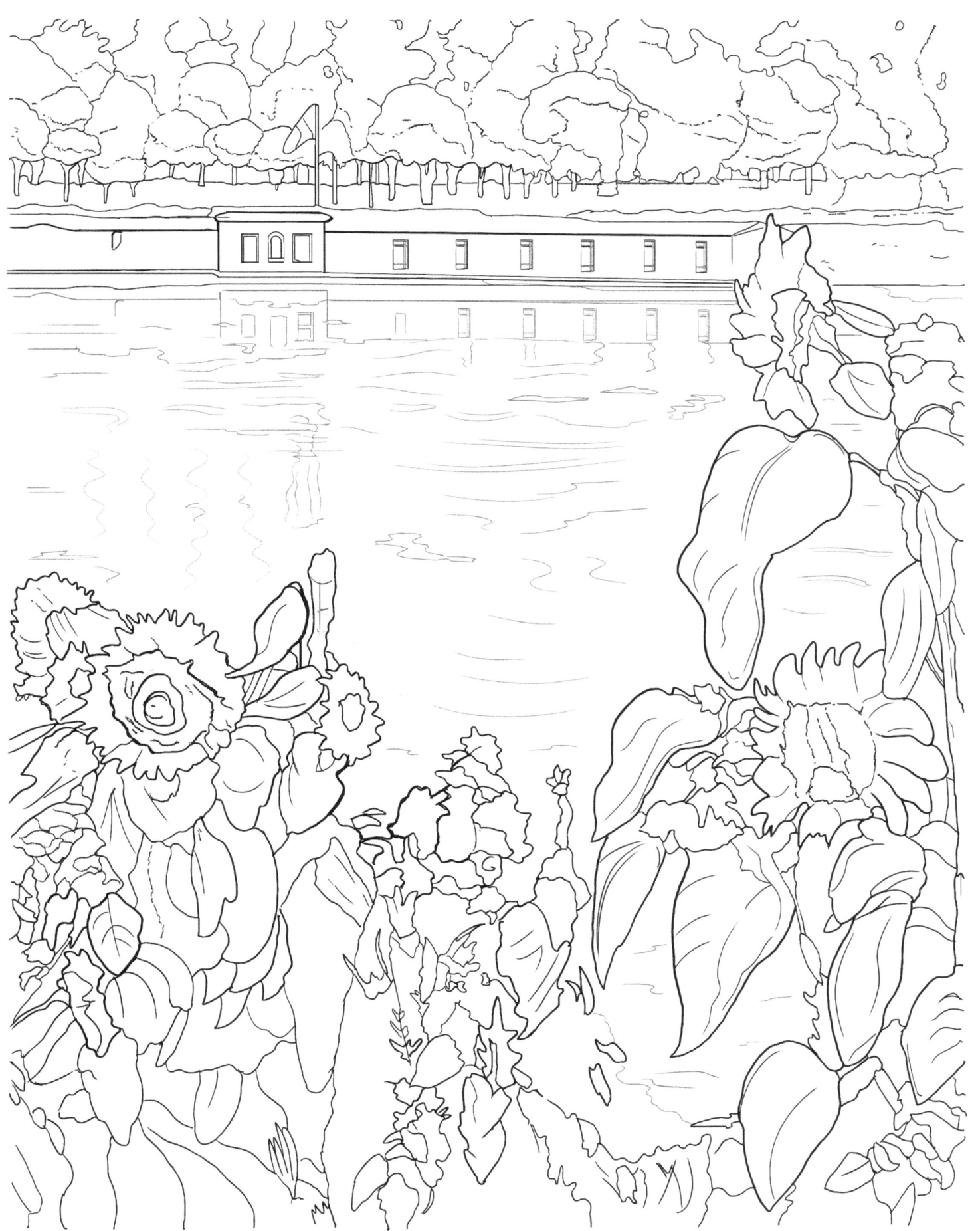

Plate 10.
Sunflowers on the banks of the Seine, 1886.

The painting depicts cheerful brightly colored sunflowers in front of a river bank. The lush and vivid sunflower heads are protagonists of this canvas, painted in thickly sensuous brushstrokes. In the background a white barge or a boat house is reflected in the water by vast horizontal brushstrokes. The tricolored French flag produces an elongated beautiful reflection in the water, along with the reflections of the green foliage and bright sunlight. The brushstrokes are dynamic and full of life. Again, as we have witnessed in Caillebotte's other landscapes, despite the non present moving human figures, the artist's swift and elongated brushstrokes and thick layers of paint are capable to animate the painting with movement and motion, creating a sense of human presence.

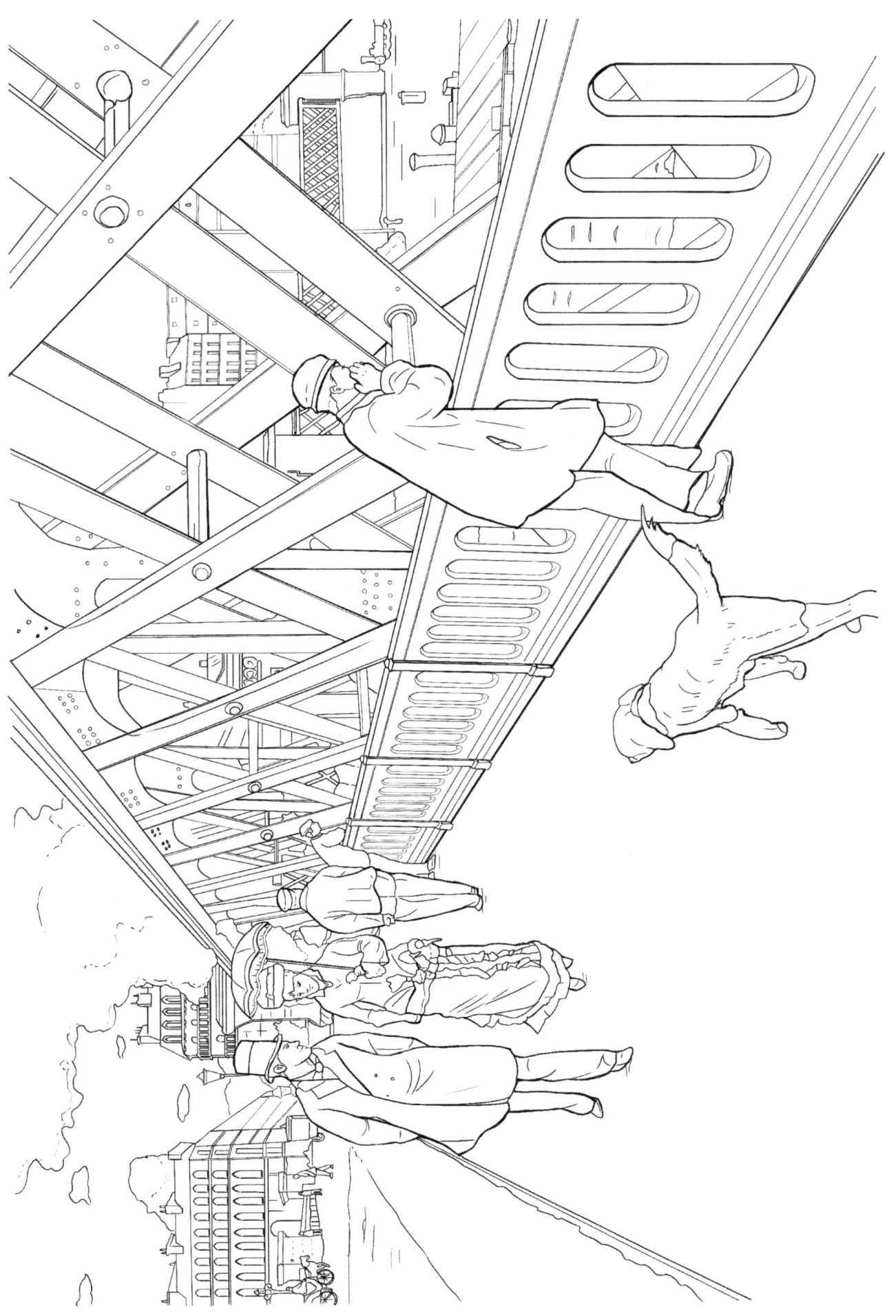

Plate 11.
On the Pont de l'Europe, 1876-77.

In this painting Caillebotte uses monochromatic and subdued steel blue colors, which seem to reflect the cold and windy evening. The artist depicts three figures, all turned away from the viewer. The men in top hats are practically mirror images of each other, dressed in identical long coats with turned up collars. This mirror technique and the cropping of one of the figures on the far left has a photographic quality. The men dressed in a similar way also remind us of the conformed modern urban society of the 19th century, which appears to be standardized and mass-produced just as the world around them.

Caillebotte uses strong diagonals and patterns to dissect the picture into equal geometric spaces. The three figures squatter in the left half of the painting to create a sense of unbalance, as if the human figures are trying to escape the predetermined and solid symmetry of modern engineering. The men standing near the bridge railing are looking at the Saint Lazare train station, a famous subject that inspired many impressionist artists. Caillebotte's friend Monet has painted over a dozen paintings of the Saint Lazare station in 1877, three variations of which were purchased by Caillebotte for his private collection.

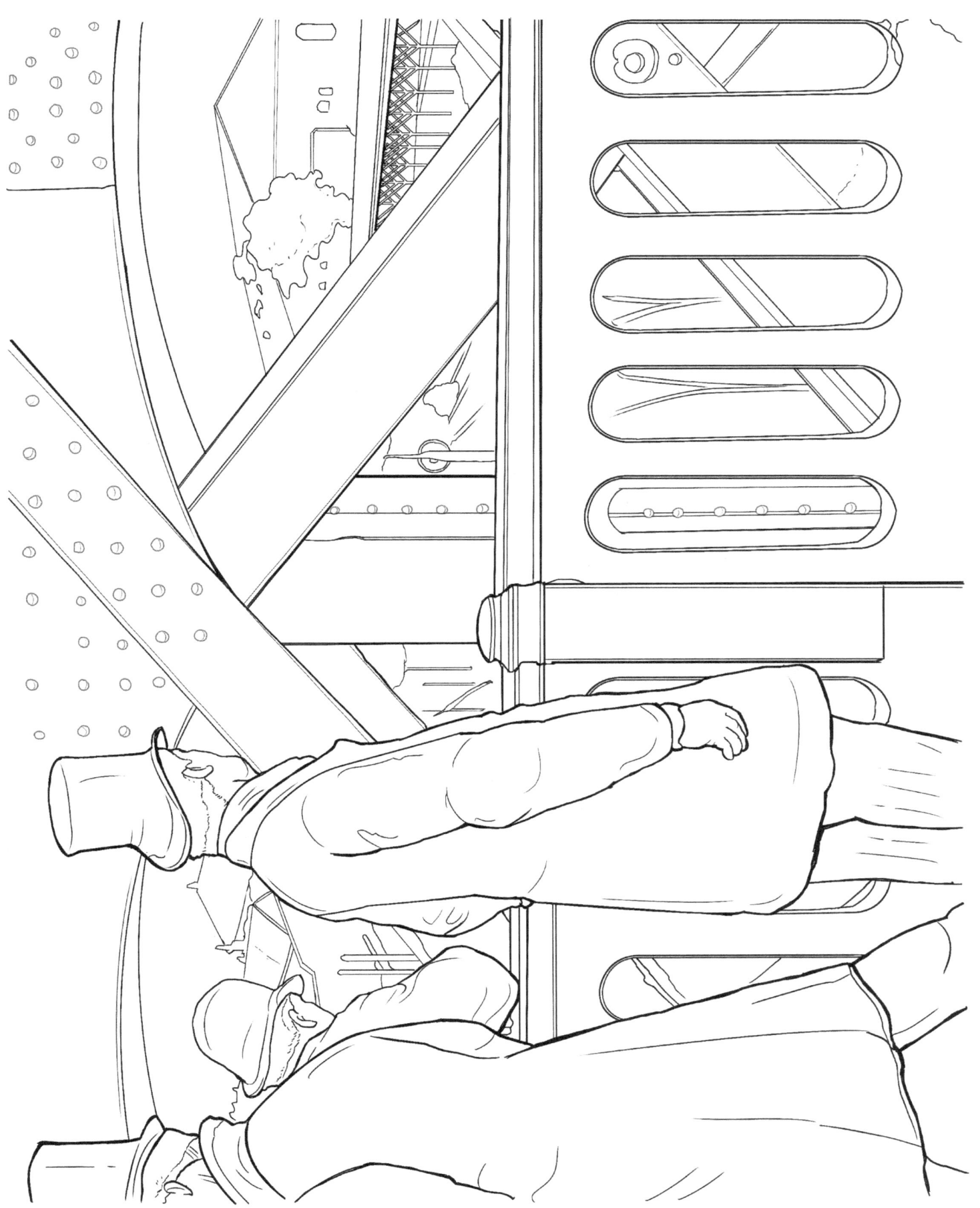

Plate 12.
The Europe Bridge (Le Pont de l'Europe), **1876.**

With the development and popularity of the railroad lines in the 19th century, the train stations started playing an important part in everyday city life. The Saint-Lazare train station was one of those modern Parisian city life spaces that have inspired many impressionists, such as Monet, by its trains submerged in steam and the atmospheric movement in the stations. Several months before the execution of the first Saint-Lazare train station, Caillebotte painted the bridge of Europe that dominates the site as a silent witness of the technological and modern engineering progress. This grand metallic bridge, completed in 1868, is situated on the Europe Square, from which radiate six streets named after the largest cities of this continent. The metallic " X " shaped beams direct the viewer's eyes to the Saint Petersburg street.

The artist is believed to have portrayed himself as the figure in a top hat who is walking towards the viewer. The young fashionably dressed woman walking slightly behind him is most likely his friend Madam Hagen. The man's gaze seemed to be focused on a young working-class man leaning against the bridge railing. The juxtaposition of social classes and their interaction is of interest to the artist, which is evident in his numerous paintings.

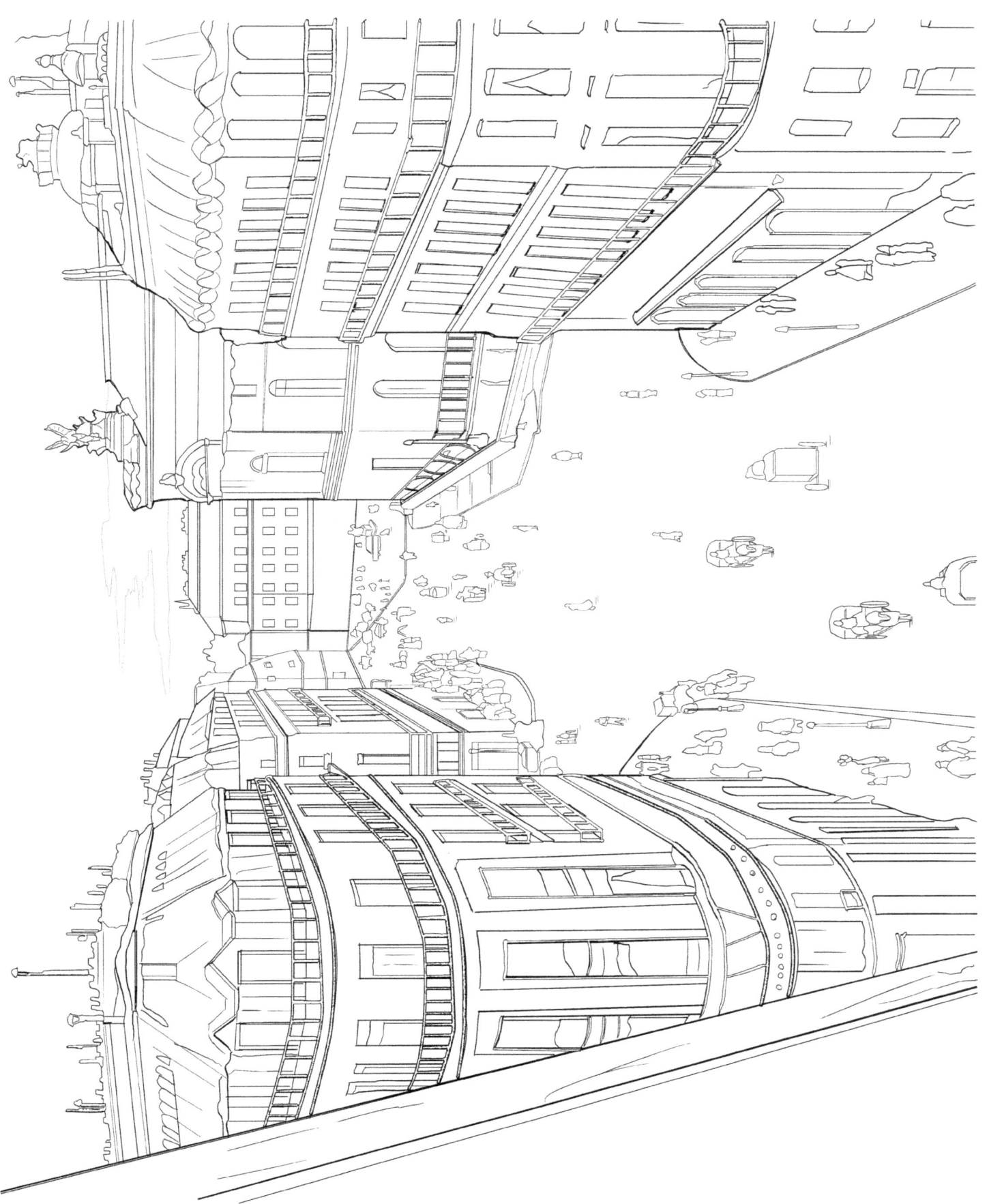

Plate 13.
Rue Halévy, Seen From the 6th Floor, 1878.

The painting shows a slightly vertiginous downward gaze unto a vast Haussmann Paris street, Rue Halevy, named after a musician Fromental Halévy, and situated in the 9th arrondissement of Paris. We can notice in the background the gold winged statues on the roofs of Palais Garnier, the famous Parisian Opera house.

Caillebotte depicts an everyday scene of the Parisian urban space from a birds eye view. This perspective is slightly dizzying to the viewer, whom the artist has placed in the first rang, and suggests certain detachment, anxiety and dispassionateness of the new urban life in a big metropolis. There are numerous people walking on the streets and carriages passing by, yet they all seem to be struggling in a disorganized motion. The blue-violet and burnt yellow colors of the tenacious and thick brushstrokes seem to add even more tension to the melancholy and nostalgia of the painting and the faceless strangers on its street.

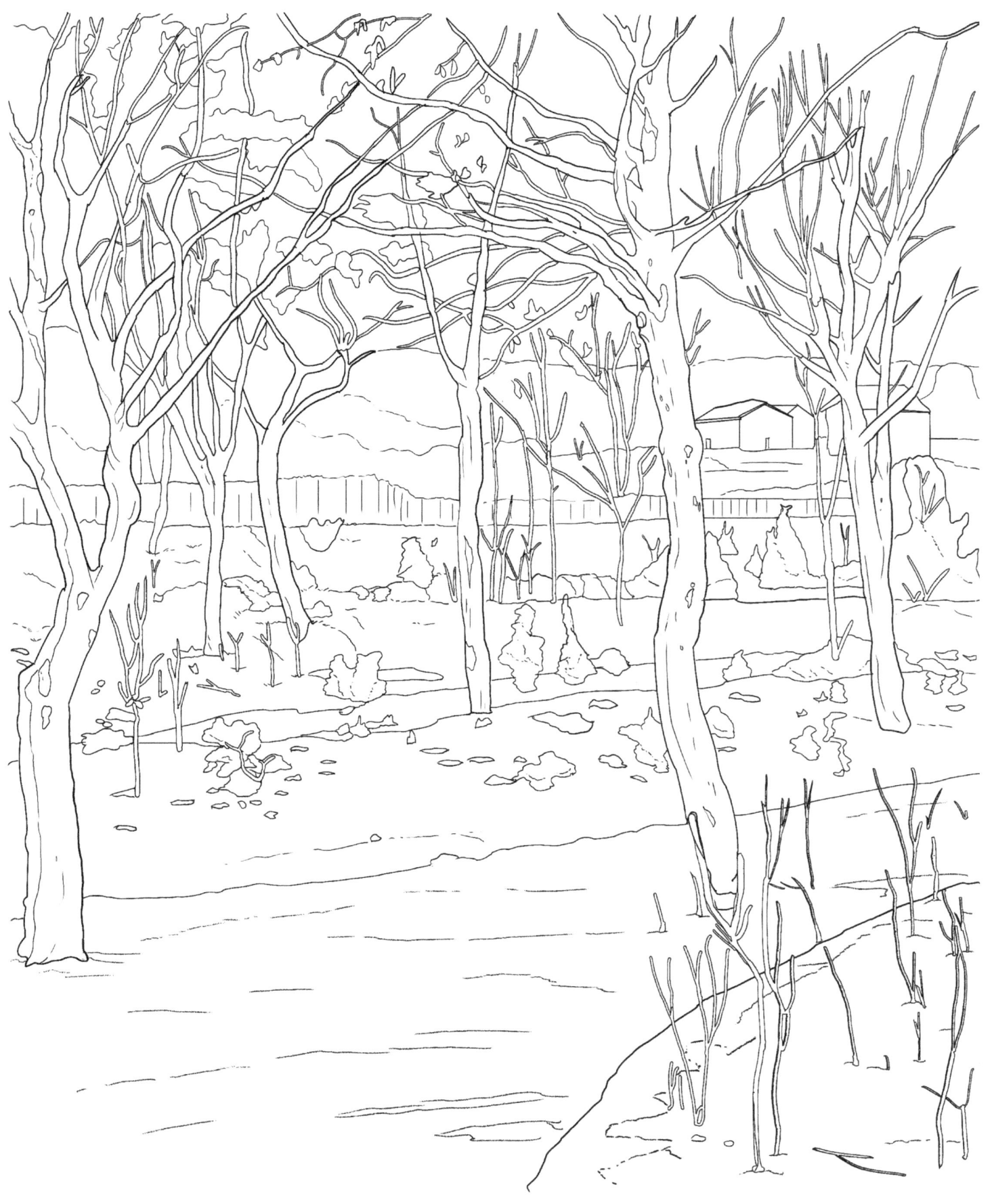

Plate 14.
The Garden at Petit Gennevilliers in Winter, 1894.

The painting depicts a winter garden landscape in the artist's estate at Petit Gennevilliers. The bare tree trunks are only slightly covered with auburn leafage and streaks of snow are seen on the ground. Yet the painting's warm earthly pastel green and red tones suggest a sunny winter day pleasant for walking outside. In the background we can notice a small red roofed house, which is most likely the artist's own estate house as it reminds one of his paintings "The Dahlias Garden at Petit Gennevilliers". Caillebotte's interest in perspective, patterns and linear movements is evident in the landscape's rows of horizontal shadows cast by the nude trees, balanced by the vertical sharp lines of the tree trunks and rose stems in the foreground.

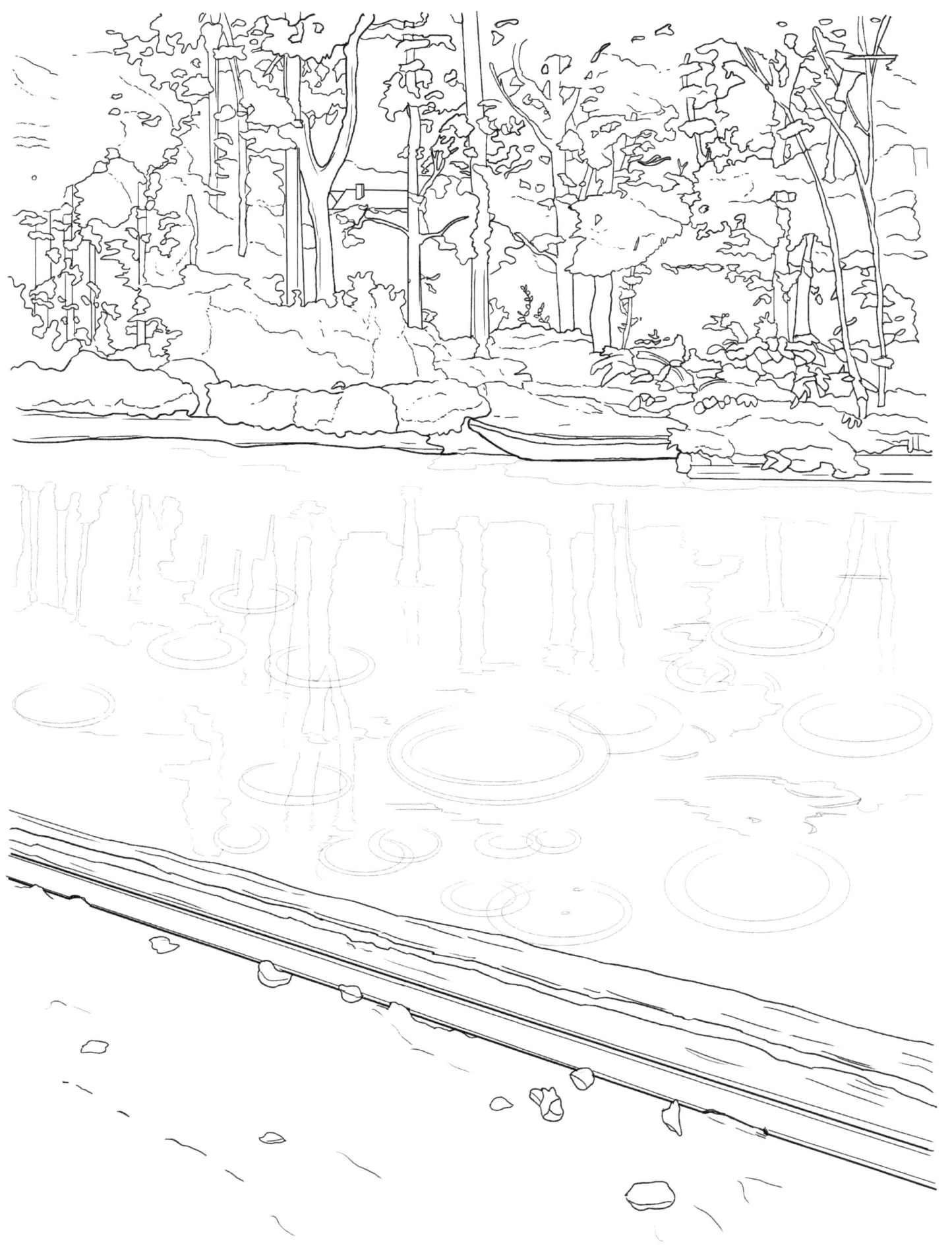

Plate 15.
Yerres, Effect of the Rain, 1875.

This painting is a beautiful and mesmerizing rain scene depicting a close-up of the Yerres river. The water reflections of the bright summer sky, horizontal tree trunks and the poetic rhythm of ripples across the water create a peaceful and calming sensation. This painting was one of the first where Caillebotte's main focus of the composition is water, its texture and its reflections, executed in smooth and thick brushstrokes. The lonely canoe quietly lingering on the river bank is reminiscent of the canoes or skiffs depicted by Caillebotte in his Boaters series. A little house with the red roof hiding in the rich summer foliage is the only suggestion of human presence in this tranquil nature scene.

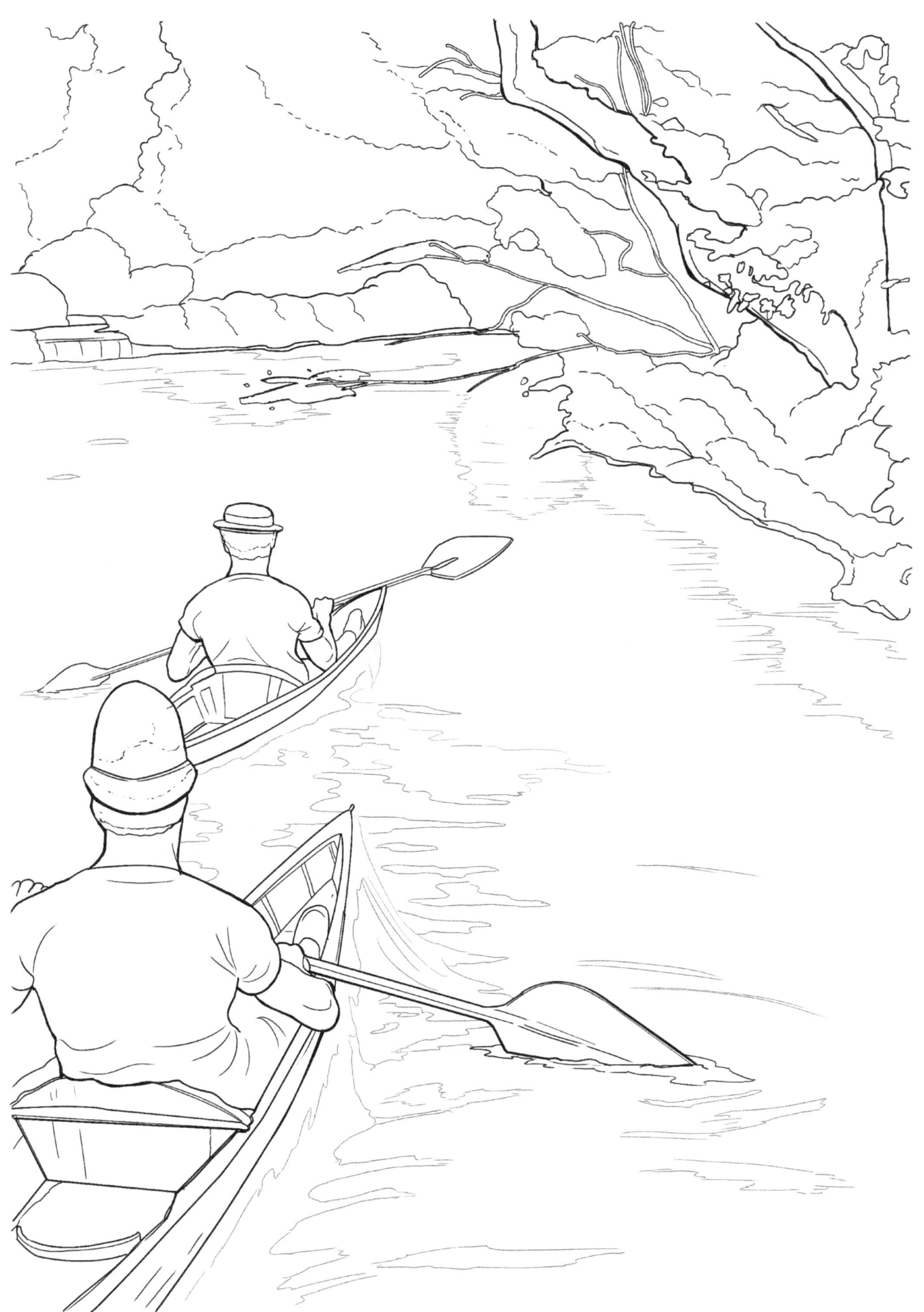

Plate 16.
Périssoires, **1878.**

Périssoires painting was presented by the artist as a triptych along with other two works depicting lively bathing and boating scenes on the Yerres river. It is yet another painting of Caillebotte's series depicting bright summer days in the artist's parents summer residency on the Yerres river, surrounded by swimmers, rowers and canoers. The theme of leisurely summer ventures continues an old artistic tradition of depicting seasonal activities, a theme which was also favored and often used by Caillebotte's friends Monet and Renoir. The two men in skiffs swiftly glide across the river, their dynamic movements are emphasized by the short and broken brushwork. The close-up of the rowing man is cut-off, a bold photographic technique often used by Caillebotte, was very contemporary and audacious at the time. standing in the corner of the crossroad, and yearning to find out more about their stories. Do they know each other? Is she waiting for him?

Caillebotte's close-up compositions create a sense of tangible proximity between the viewer and the foreground figure, as if inviting the viewer to step into the personal space of the painting's protagonist. This technique places the viewer in the place of the main figure, creating a desire to find out more about his story, thoughts and life.

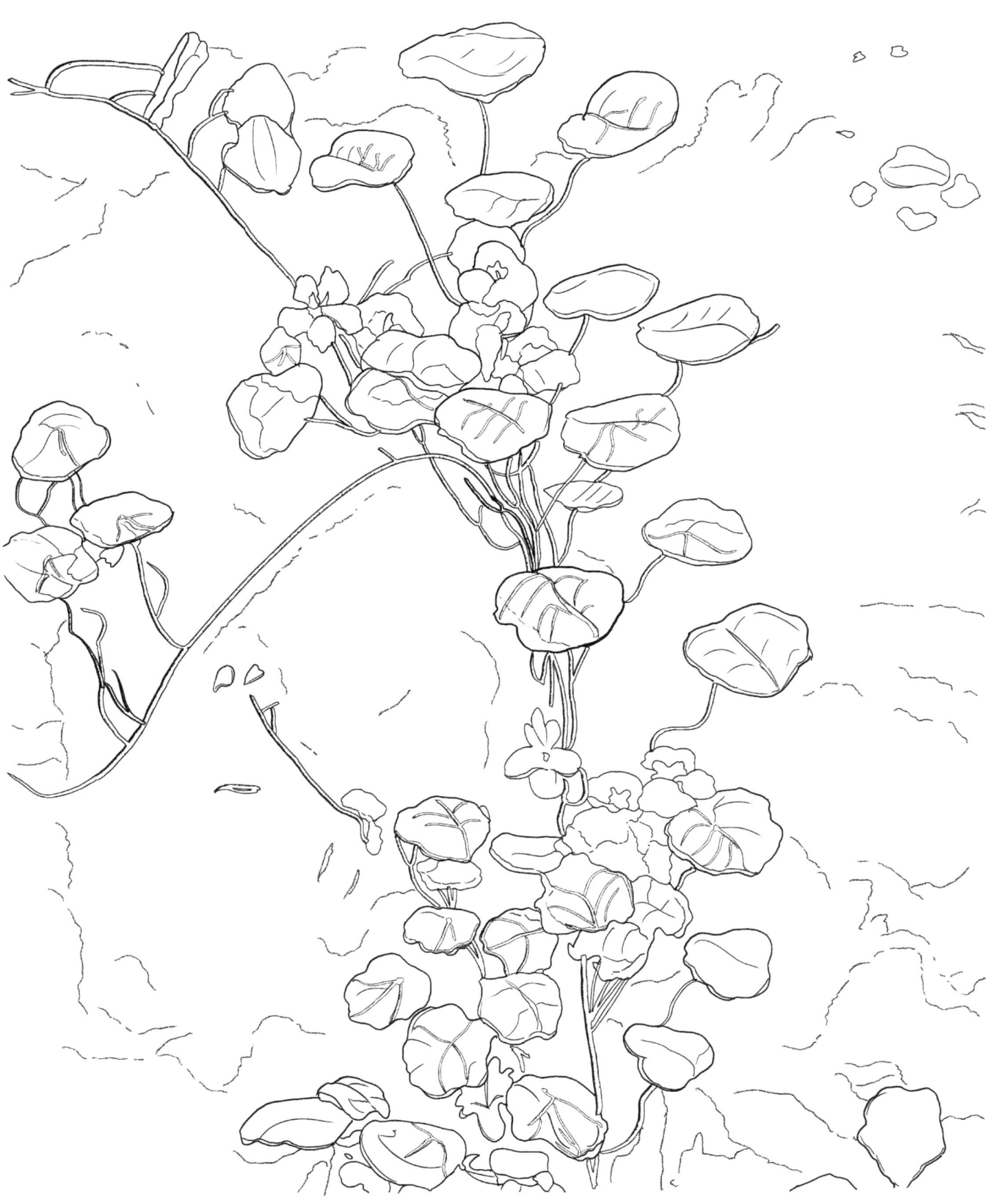

Plate 17.
Nasturtiums, **1892.**

The painting depicts the artist's enduring fascination with garden flowers. A blooming nasturtiums plant flowers and leaves joyfully climb up a wall. The climbing flowers were most likely grown in one of the Caillebotte's summer residences, as nasturtiums are annual garden flowers with vibrant colors and green leaves that are edible and easy to grow. The artist painted different versions of the nasturtiums, depicting the climbing flowers set against different colored backgrounds. This painting is set against a warm earthly toned wall, the brushstrokes are light and rhythmic, creating a sensation that the flowers are almost floating on water rather than climbing up a wall.

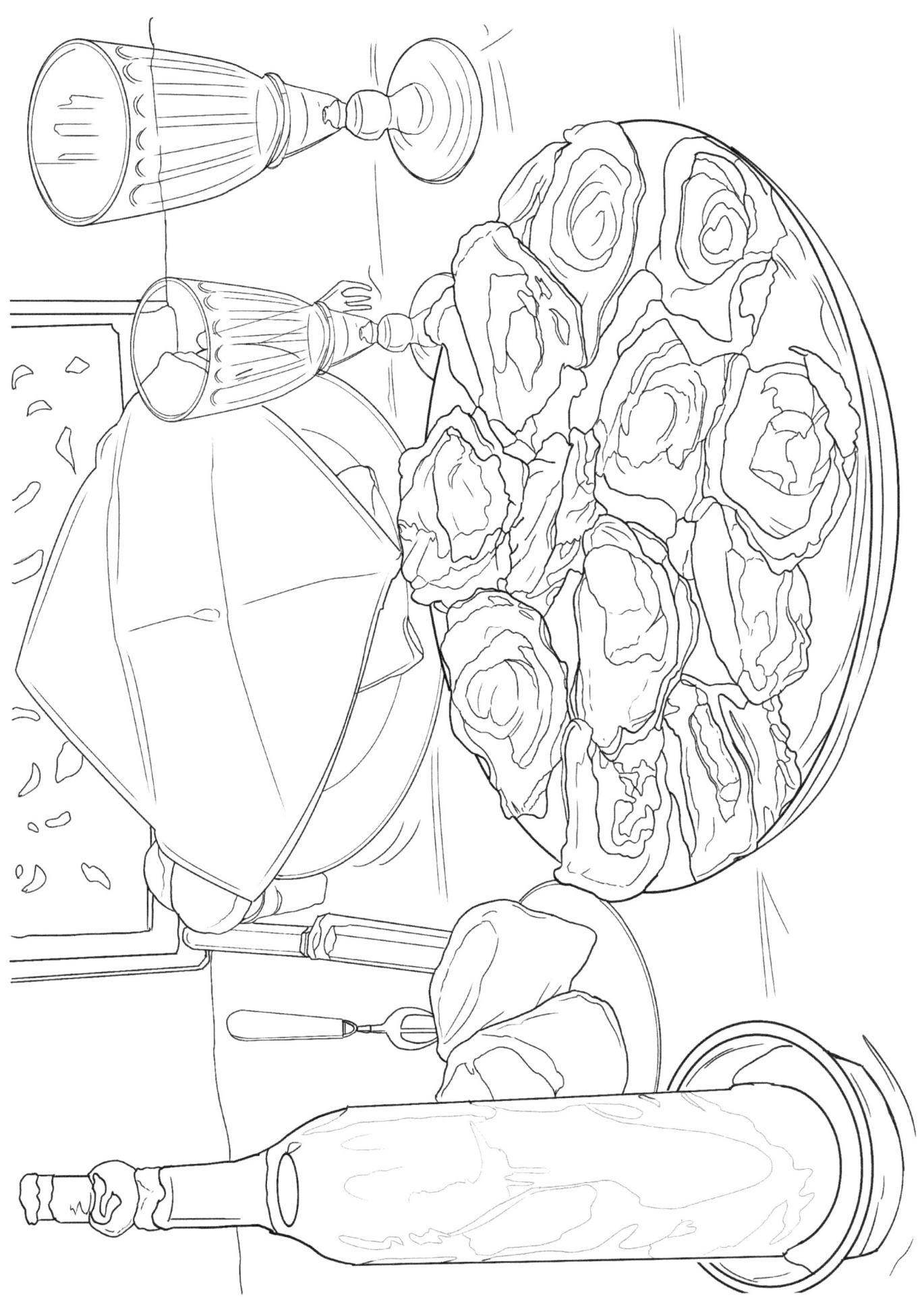

Plate 18.
Still Life with Oysters, **1881.**

This still life depicting oysters and lemons, perennially poised in time, is reminiscent of the realistic Dutch still life paintings of the 17th century. Oysters were traditionally a symbol of lust and appear in numerous Dutch paintings alongside carefully carved lemons and a luxurious goblet of wine. One can suggest that at the time Caillebotte mastered his still life composition techniques, he drew his inspiration from the old still life masters such as Jan van de Velde and Pieter Claesz, known for their magnificent oyster and lemons arrangements. The bottle and the wine glasses in Caillebotte's painting provide strong vertical elements that balance the horizontal rows of the oyster shells and the horizontal creases of the table cloth and the table napkin folds.

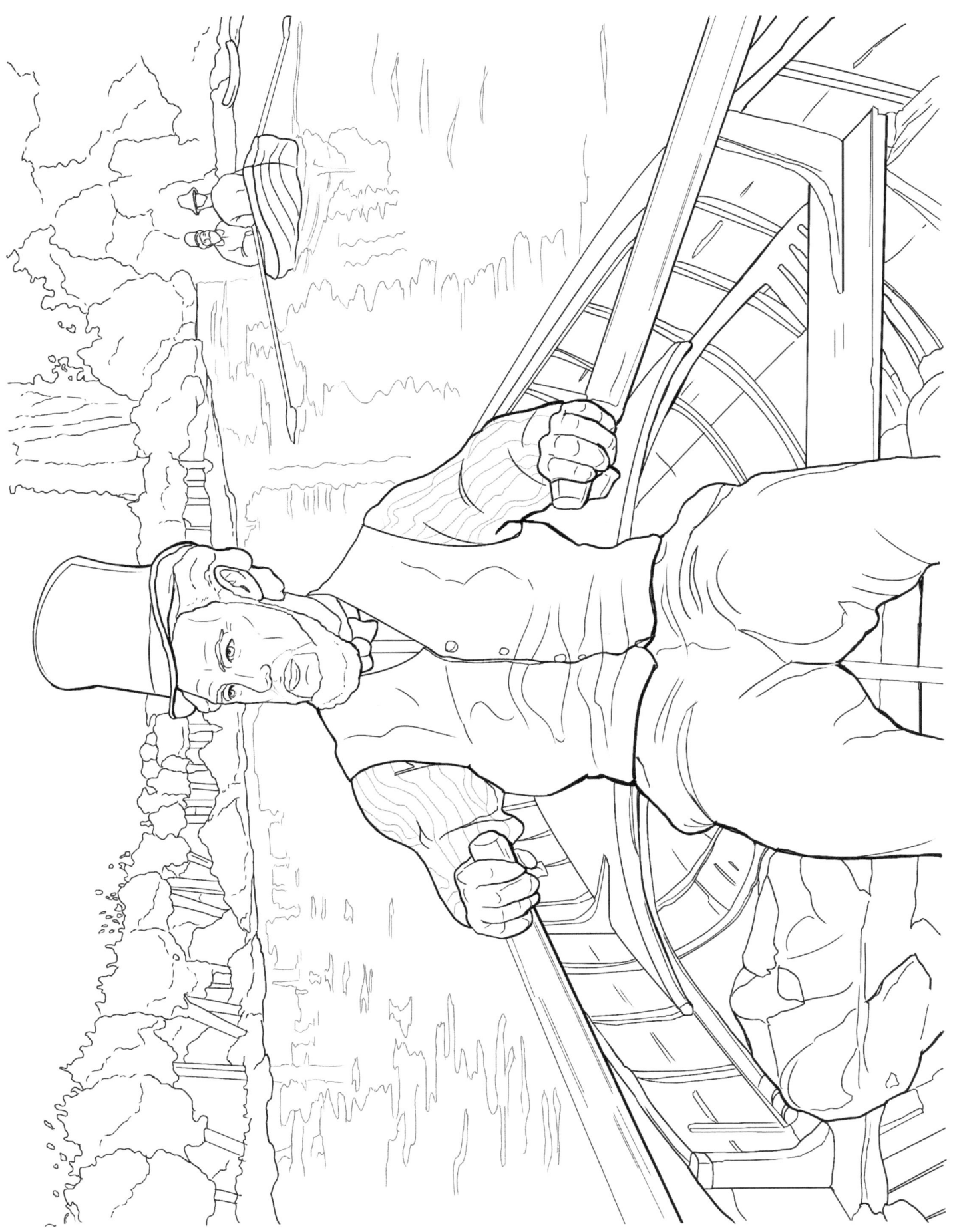

Plate 19.
Boating Party, 1877-1878.

This painting depicting a rowing man in a top hat, also known as *Oarsman in a Top Hat*, belongs to the series of seven paintings of boatmen by Caillebotte. The composition of the painting is cinematic; in the movie industry it is referred to as "the subjective camera". In this close spatial arrangement, the artist (or the spectator) becomes a part of the action, by being seated facing the figure represented in *Boating Party*. This tromp-l'oeil effect was most likely inspired by Caillebotte's avid interest in the advances of photography as an art form, and by the invention of wide-angle photographic lenses since 1860's.

The close-up perspective of the rower and the boat shows a great sense of movement. The boat is slightly tilted and man's right hand is higher than the left one, highlighting the sense of continuous motion. The man in the foreground is painted in a very detailed and realistic style, with an apparent photographic quality in his facial expression, his clothing and the details of the boat. The background and the water with green foliage reflections and bright reflections of light are executed in a more impressionistic style with fragmented loose brushwork and light colors.

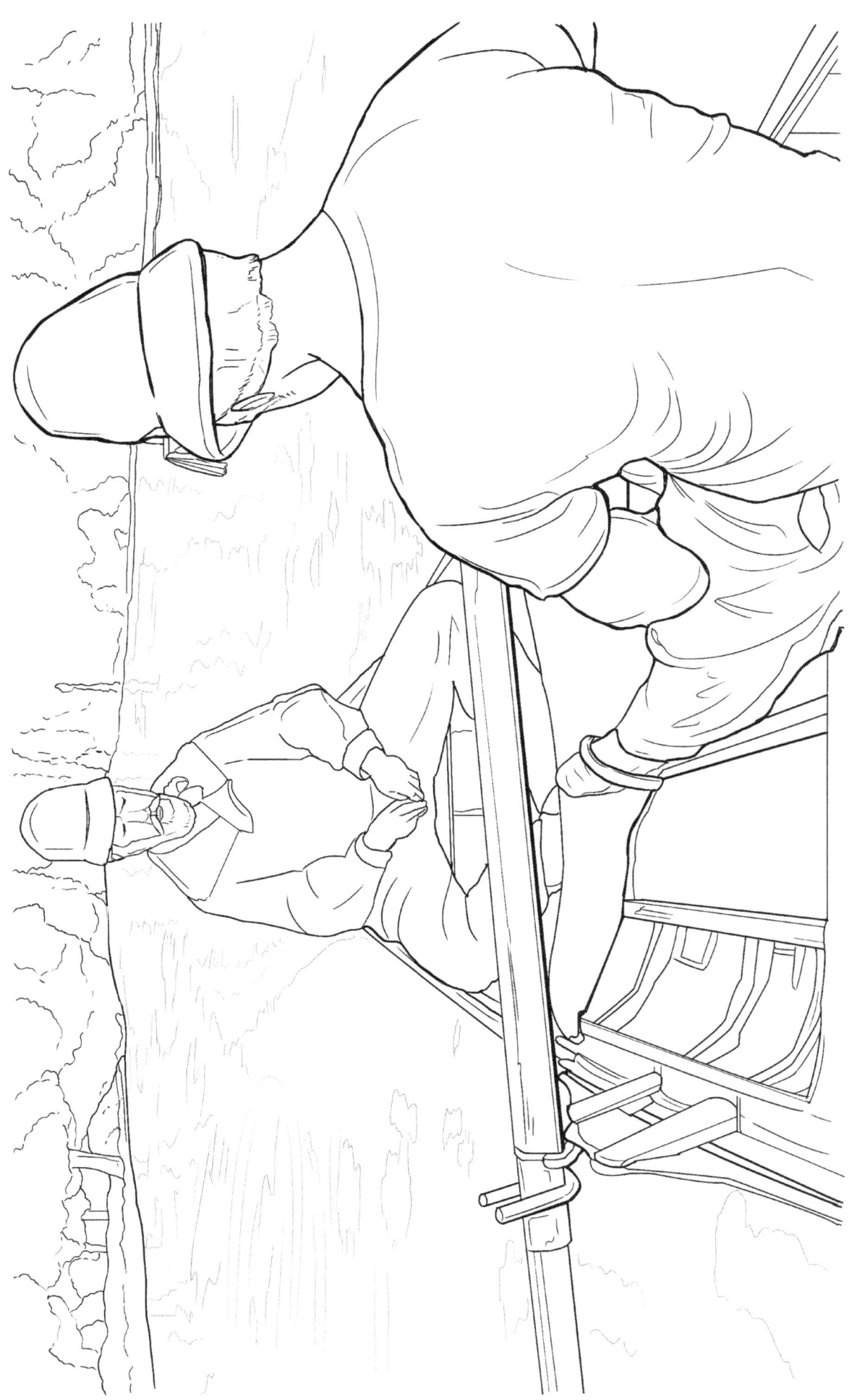

Plate 20.
Boaters on the Yerres, **1877.**

This boating scene on the quiet Yerres river belongs to a series of the seven boating scenes which the artist painted between 1877 and 1877, in his family estate at Yerres. The rowing boaters, smoothly gliding on the water in one-man skiffs, known as "périssoires" were a great subject matter for Caillebotte to study the human figure in motion. The lively water splashes and foliage reflections allowed the artist to play with colors and the light reflection effects in the transparent water. The most space of the painting is given to water which is painted in vast and horizontal brushstrokes.

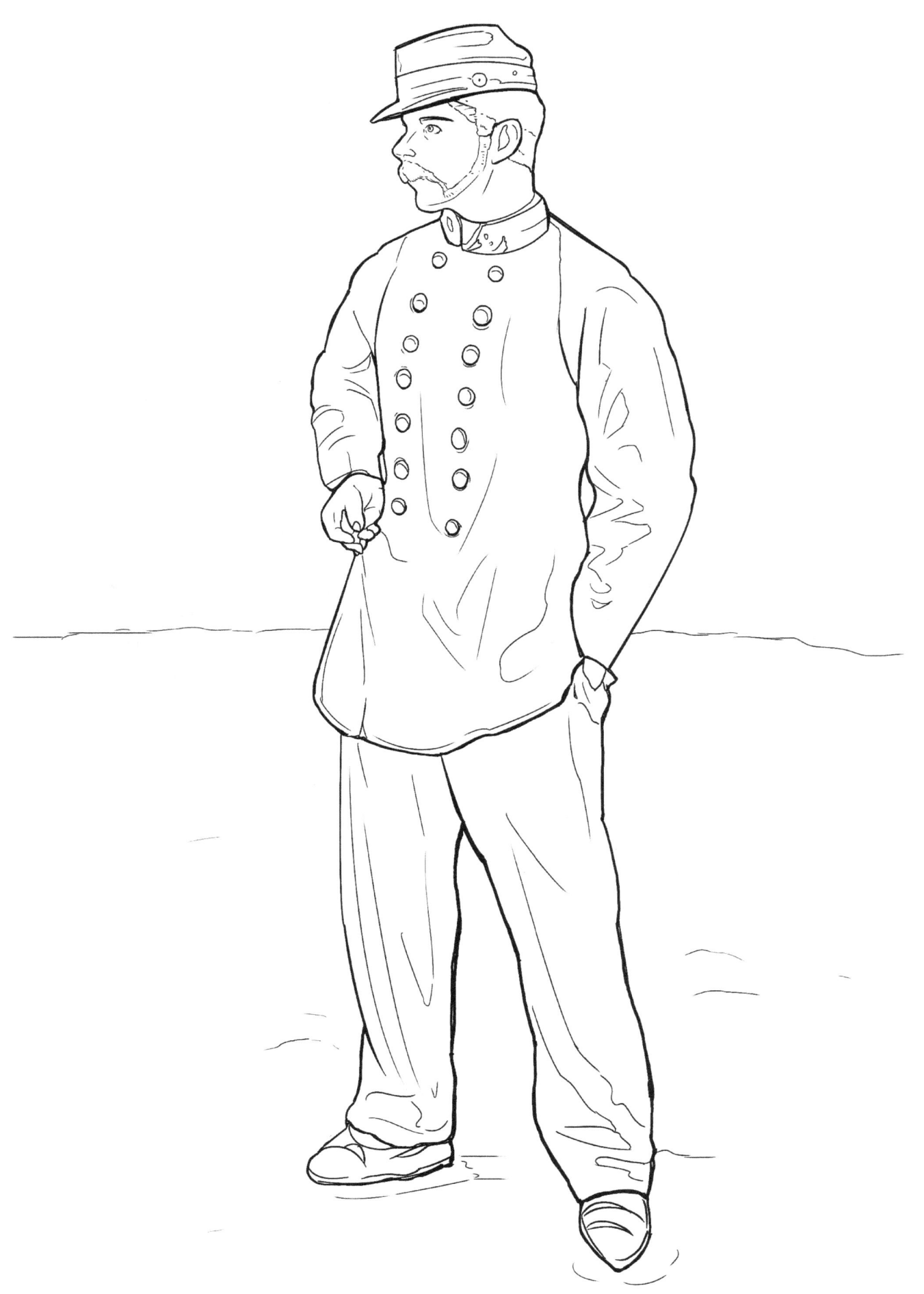

Plate 21.
A Soldier, **1881.**

The painting depicts a French soldier wearing a uniform in vibrant colors, scarlet red trousers and a vivid blue coat. Caillebotte executed this portrait in thick and textured brushwork, with detailed attention to the intensity of brilliant uniform colors and reflection effects on the two rows of gold buttons and on the standing collar. This strikingly bright and conspicuous color palette might seem surprising considering the contemporary drab camouflage and subdued khaki colored uniforms with disruptive patterns. In the beginning of the 19th century during the Napoleonic wars, the French military, notably those in the Imperial Guard, were considered to own the most distinctive uniforms of the time. A possible reason for those ostentatious uniforms was that the French army was supposed to be recognized as the grand conquerors of many nations, the colors of their uniforms reflecting the boldness of the army. The bright color palette remained until the First World War when more subdued and less expensive uniforms were adopted for the active service.

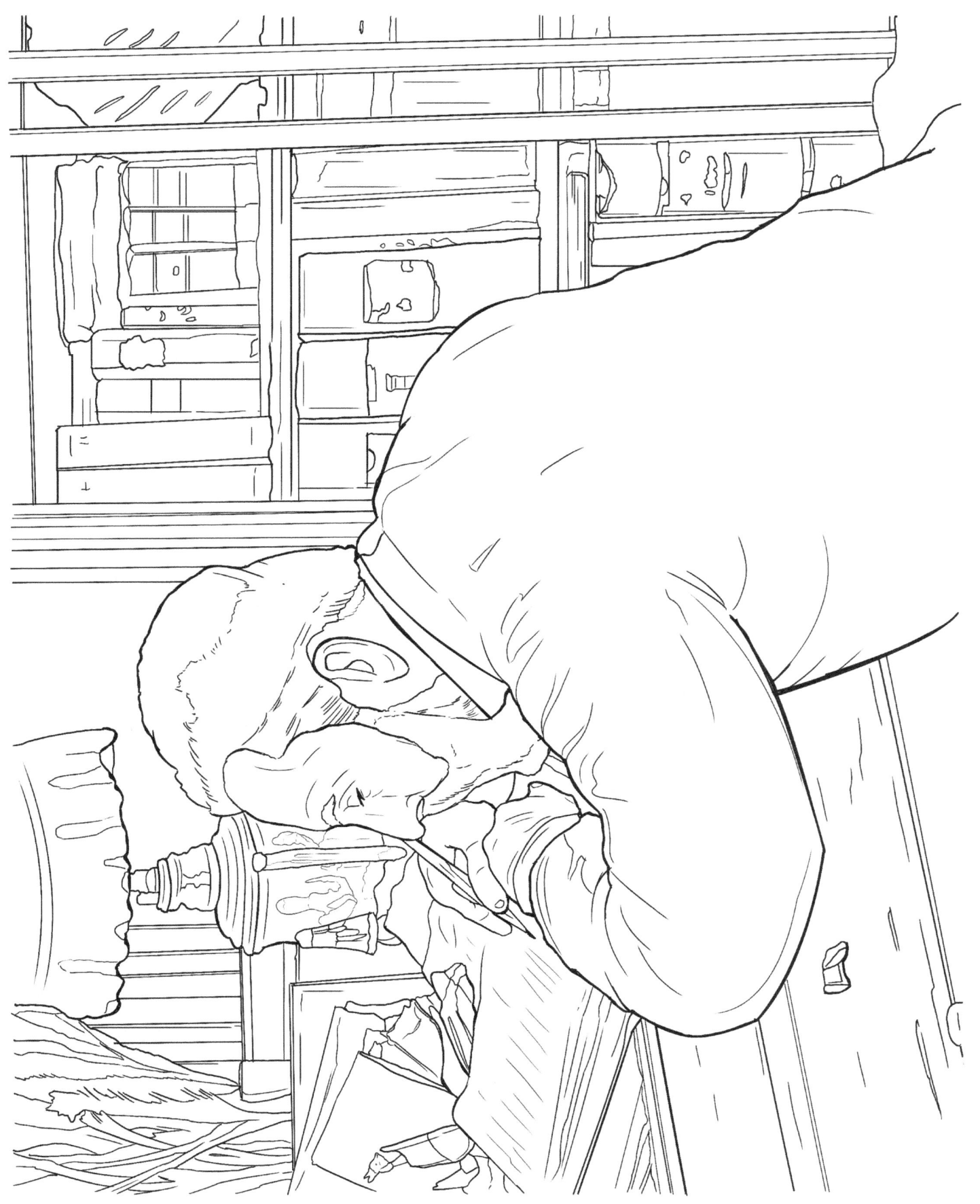

Plate 22.
Portrait of Henri Cordier, **1883.**

Henri Cordier, the artist's good friend, was a French author, historian, ethnographer and linguist, who has been working in China and serving as the President of the Geography Society. In this portrait, Henri is half-turned to the viewer, lost in pensive thoughts. Caillebotte portrays Cordier as a true intellectual modern man, surrounded by numerous books, his gaze fully immersed in writing in the intimacy of his study room. The books taking up almost half of the pictorial space symbolize the profession of the bibliophile protagonist, as do the fuzzy quill pens painted with great attention to detail. Henri Cordier's head is painted in lighter bright colors, as if to concentrate the viewer's attention on the mind process of the erudite man fully concentrated in his thoughts.

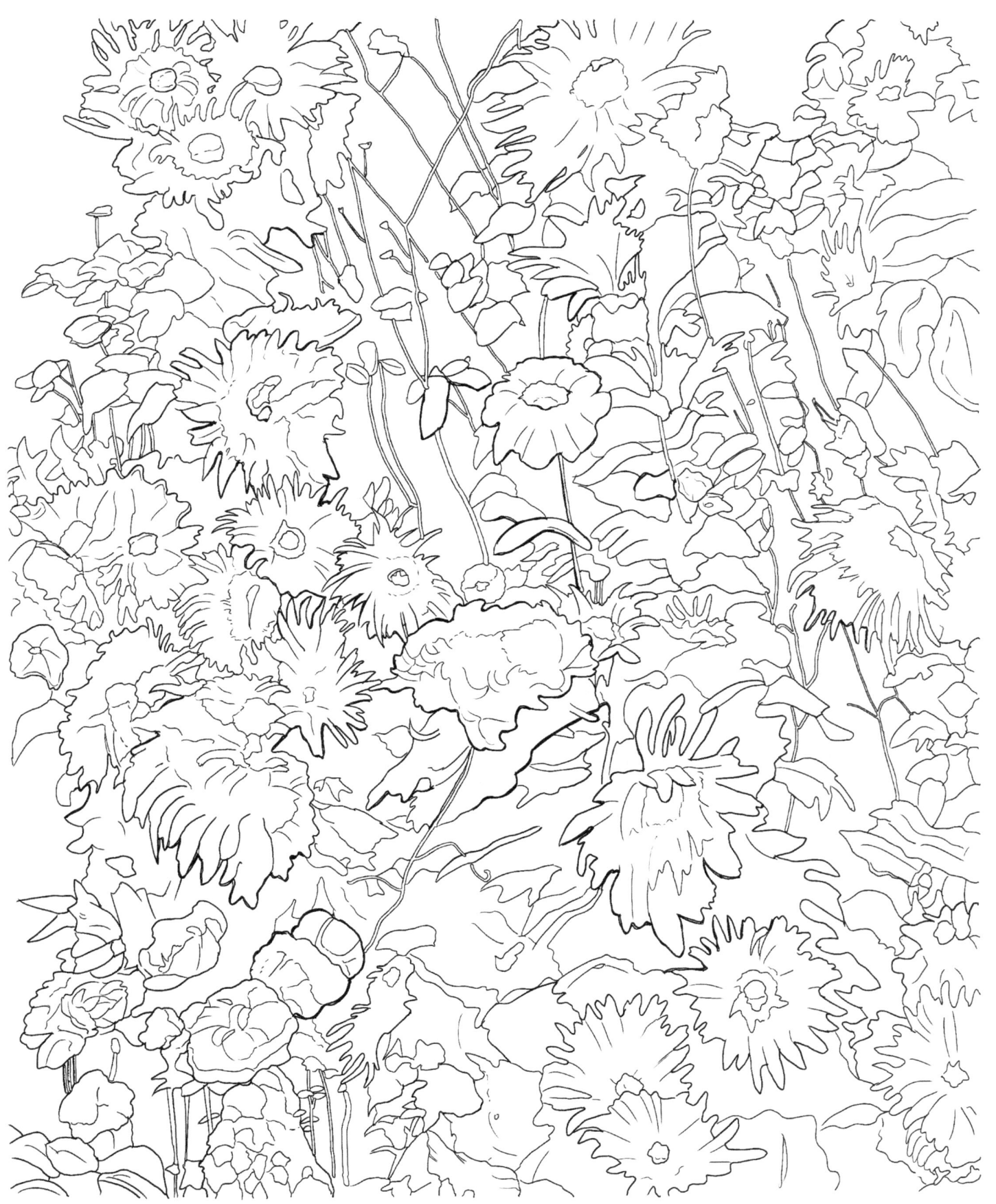

Plate 23.
White and Yellow Chryanthemums, 1893.

This flower garden scene is most likely based on flowers the artist himself cultivated at his private property in the gardens at Petit Gennevilliers. This painting is one of the numerous floral still lifes that the artist started to execute around 1880's when the interest in the still life genre began to rekindle. Chrysanthemums were highly popular in France because of their luxurious and deep colors. Moreover, these flowers were highly respected for their associations with the exotic Far East and Japonism, a European late 19-th century infatuation and craze for Japanese art, which had a huge influence on the Impressionist artists.

The painting depicts the flowers in an unusual focus point and close-up view showing a dense sea of magnificent lush blossoms. This painting has been associated with the artist's project of paintings with floral images, destined for dining room decorations, alike the concept of decorative series with images of plants that Monet displayed in his house at Giverny.

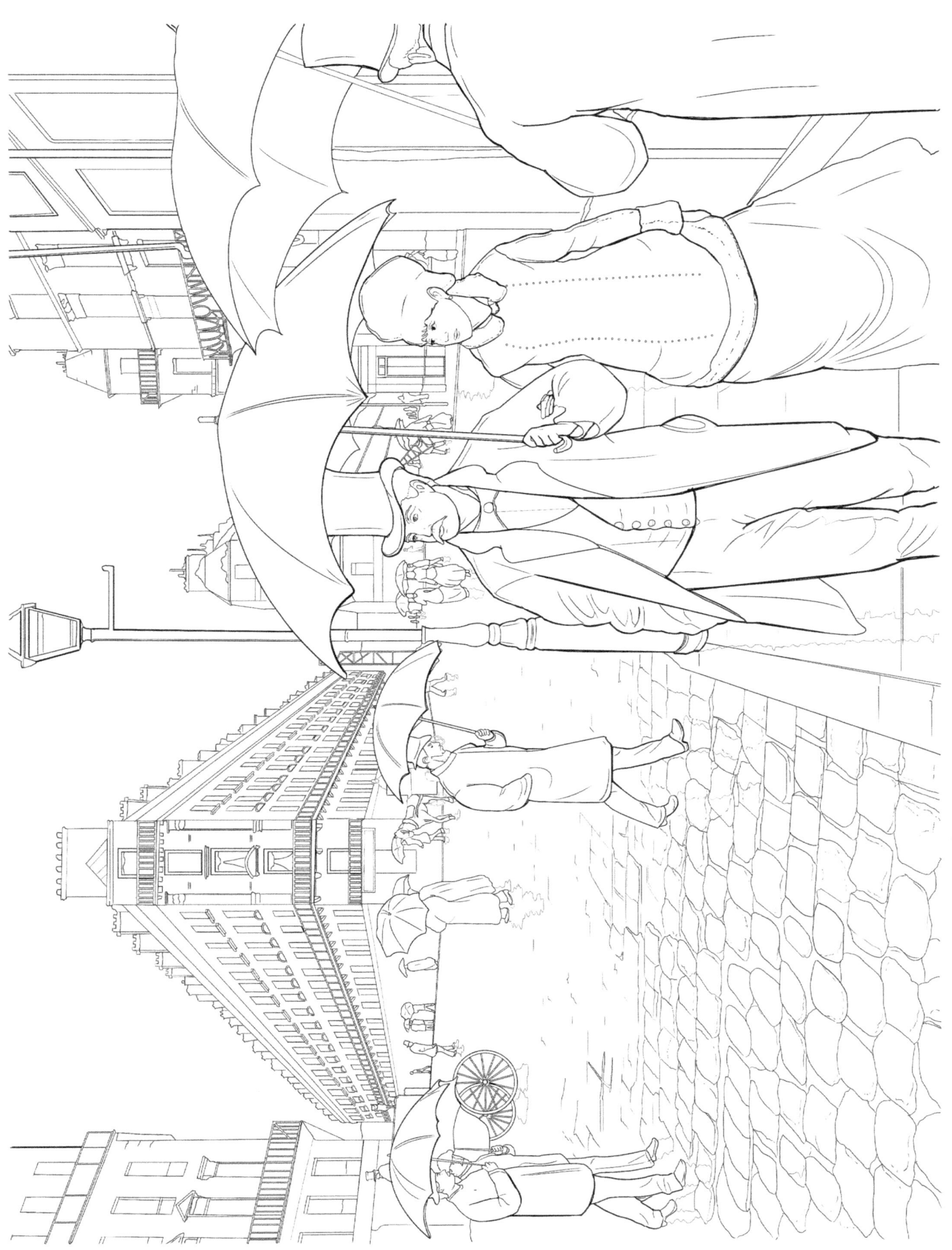

Plate 24.
Paris Street Rainy Day, 1877.

The artist is widely recognized for his realistic landscape paintings depicting urban Parisian streets and upper-class home settings of the 19th century. One of Caillebotte's most known work, "Paris Street : Rainy Day". In this work Gustave portrays a typical rainy day in the center of Paris, masterfully playing with the effects of light, shadows and wet reflections on the ground and on passer-by umbrellas. The artist uses flat and subdued pastel colors, the brushstrokes are careful, and unlike the massive brushstrokes of his fellow impressionist artists, we can see vivid lines and contours. Yet the overall feeling is light and effervescent.

The scene is very modern, showing wide and vast boulevards and new apartment buildings in Haussmann style. This was the era of Haussmann's renovation of Paris, when numerous medieval crowded neighborhoods were demolished and in its place rose the vast new squares and wide networks of boulevards. The painting depicts an intersection close to the Saint Lazare station. One may say the painting is also an intersection of social classes, which was a very modern and controversial theme at the time. In the foreground we see three upper-class figures who are very elegantly and fashionably dressed. The man on the right is cut off, a new technique reminiscent of the cropped photographs. In the background we can notice little figures belonging to a lower Parisian social class, those of a painter holding a ladder and a *bonne de chambre* opening up her umbrella.

ABOUT THE ARTIST

Gustave Caillebotte (1848-1894) was a French artist who quit the realism school of Beaux Arts de Paris to work in open space and follow the Impressionist movement. Inspired by both realism and impressionism styles, Caillebotte can be considered as one of the first Neo Impressionist artists, a movement that followed impressionism.

Caillebotte was not solely a remarkable and talented artist, experimenting with styles and new art techniques, but an important art collector and a patron of the impressionist movement. Caillebotte devoted a part of his fortune inherited from his father, a judge of the Seine Tribunal, to support the art work of his friends. After his rather early death in his 40's, the artist has left an important collection of works of his artist friends and his own paintings to the French State, which can now be seen in the impressionism Museum d'Orsay in Paris.